GREAT OPPORTUNITIES INSIDE DIFFICULTIES

DISCOVERING FAITH THAT WORKS

GREAT OPPORTUNITIES INSIDE DIFFICULTIES

DISCOVERING FAITH THAT WORKS

RUE P. STEWART

Great Opportunities Inside Difficulties

Copyright © 2021 Rue P. Stewart

ISBN: 978-1-946702-54-8

All rights reserved. No part of this book may be reproduced or transmitted in any form or by any means, electronic or mechanical, including photocopying, recording, or by any information storage and retrieval system, without permission in writing from the author.

Published by Freeze Time Media

Special thanks to:

My wife, Irena, for making my life rich and joyful.

The people who helped me complete this book, including Derek, who supported and encouraged me; Monika, for her skill and editing talent; and Di Freeze and Freeze Time Media, my publisher.

The artists at Shutterstock and Unsplash, whose photos brought my book to life, and Lisa Shifren Photography for the cover photo.

Most of all, to God, for my past, my future, the path that has been laid out in front of me, which included me writing this book, and for placing the people above and others in my life. I am profoundly grateful.

I dedicate this book to anyone willing to believe in the oftentimes inconceivable great purpose that lies within even the most difficult of circumstances and in the ego-deflating reality that: "we know infinitely little," that a "truly loving, unfathomable God" loves us all, and that there is a mind-blowing beautiful answer to the questions of "Why are we here?" and "Why did we have to go through everything that we did?"

Contents

Author's Preface	xi
Introduction	xiii
Story 1: Embracing Hope	1
Losing Hope	2
Car Accident	3
Before The Accident	5
Strange Behavior	10
Hope	21
Willingness	34
Action	40
Story 2: A Real Connection	47
Belief	48
Story 3: Learning to Love Myself	59
Courage	60
Story 4: Grace I Couldn't See	69
Visualization	70
Story 5: Surrendering to Success	81
Publishing this Book	82
Acceptance	84
Humility	87
Responsibility	91
Trust	93
Surrender	97
Closing	101
About the Author	105

Author's Preface

I am writing this book in an attempt to give someone hope in the same way I was given hope when I was going through some difficult times in my life. Since I embraced hope, that evening over twenty-six years ago, my world has changed entirely, and I keep finding a faith that works. May you, the reader, find some story or phrase in this book that inspires you to overcome the challenges you are currently facing and to create a new life worth living.

Know that you can.

Introduction

"What if ... we had a guarantee that the problem bothering us would be worked out in the most perfect way, and at the best possible time. ...
What if three years from now we'd be grateful for that problem, and its solution.
What if ... we had a guarantee that everything that is happening and has happened in our life was meant to be, planned just for us, and in our best interest."

- Melody Beattie

I was in a twelve-step meeting at a community center when I first heard someone read this passage above. These words filled me with hope and a deep sense of purpose. I left the meeting, got in my car, and started driving. Not long after I was driving, I was overcome with strong feelings and began crying. I don't cry often, so this was a strange experience. The first thought I had after I started crying was how beautiful God's love must be ... for God to love me so much that there is meaning, purpose, and a pre-orchestrated great benefit

Great Opportunities Inside Difficulties

in the middle of the most difficult challenges I must walk through in life.

In this book, I will discuss eleven principles of a faith that works. These principles are Hope, Willingness, Action, Belief, Courage, Visualization, Acceptance, Humility, Responsibility, Trust, and Surrender. I have discovered these concepts of faith in having to walk through five difficult challenges in my life. These challenges include losing hope while suffering from a head injury, with mental illness, addiction, and being incarcerated; passing the bar exam to become a lawyer; dating before I met my wife; starting my own law practice; and publishing this book. From walking through these five challenges, I've discovered these eleven concepts of faith and the realization that there are great opportunities inside difficult problems.

"In the midst of difficulty lies opportunity."

– Albert Einstein

Story 1
Embracing Hope

Losing Hope

"Don't lose hope.
When the sun goes down, the stars come out."

– **B. Crouch**

The first difficult challenge I had to walk through in life that showed me that great opportunities exist inside of difficult problems involves me losing hope while suffering from a head injury, with mental illness, addiction, and being incarcerated. To explain this further, I need to tell you a little more about myself.

Car Accident

In the summer of 1987, I was looking forward to the fall and returning for my second year at Towson State University in Maryland.

One evening in August, I got dressed up in a sharp-looking outfit, tan from time at the beach and my summer job, and headed off to attend a party. I wasn't drinking, but I was looking forward to drinking and having fun at the party.

I remember driving down the road near my house, but I don't remember anything after that. I was told I had a head-on collision with another car and that we were both near the center lane when we collided. I had cardiac arrest and was

Great Opportunities Inside Difficulties

flown to the Shock Trauma Hospital at the University of Maryland. It was explained to me that I had a head injury, almost died, and was in a coma for several days. I stayed in the hospital for three weeks and three days. My parents visited me every day, traveling an hour and a half each way. Many friends from high school and college came to visit as well.

I was in the hospital so long because the doctors were trying to figure out where to send me because of my head injury. They looked at sending me to a head trauma center, but I was fortunate enough to keep improving. Eventually, I left the hospital, went home to my parents' house, attended occupational therapy, and went to church. After some time, I completed therapy and went back to school at the local community college.

At first, it was hard for me to reconnect with friends my age and with partying. I was still trying to make sense of how my life could change so quickly without me having any say over it. Despite this, after two years I was able to start school back at Towson State. Things were going well. I was now applying myself towards my schoolwork, getting good grades, working part-time, and was having fun with friends there. However, as I look back on my life at this time, I can see that I was beginning to do some strange things that weren't like me.

Before The Accident

Me in third grade at Idlewild Elementary School (1976)

So, what was my life like before the accident and before college?

I was born on the Eastern Shore of Maryland to two loving parents. I grew up in a middle-class home and had everything I needed and many of the things I wanted. The area in which I grew up was somewhat affluent and I was afforded many opportunities that other people are not, though I didn't realize that at the time.

Great Opportunities Inside Difficulties

In the midst of my good circumstances, there were also challenges. My dad struggled with alcoholism. My mom faced emotional and mental health problems from her childhood, and my sister and brother, who are eight and six years older than me, struggled with abusing drugs and alcohol. Even though my sister now has a college degree, and my brother has a master's license in his trade, neither completed high school. I spent my middle school years driving around with my mom, trying to find my brother and sister, and then visiting them at treatment centers.

Since I was the youngest child, had done well in high school, stayed busy playing sports, and had not gotten into any trouble, I could have been viewed as the shining star of the family. However, I was lazy and wasn't taking advantage of opportunities that were right in front of me. I had tested well on the national scholastic tests given to middle school students. As a result, the summer before eighth grade, a handful of students and I were selected to take the Scholastic Aptitude Test (SAT), given in preparation for admission to college. Based on the score we achieved on the SAT test, we would be given the opportunity to participate in a summer gifted and talented program at Johns Hopkins University.

I remember being selected to take the SAT test made me feel smart and like I had a lot of potential. However, the only preparation I did to do well on the SAT test was to contact the mother of a friend of mine to help tutor me. Then I only met with her once and never followed through on doing any other preparation. I felt mostly confused taking the SAT test, didn't do well, and the opportunity I was given for the summer gifted and talented program was limited.

That following year, my middle school started the first Highly Able classes for eighth grade. A handful of students and I were fortunate to be placed in all five of the Highly Able classes offered. I got straight C's in these classes. It wasn't because the work was too hard or too easy for me. It was because I didn't care to work hard enough to do any better. I was using my time to be an attention-seeking thirteen-year-old.

I had fun in high school hanging out with my friends and playing sports. My two biggest fears were being petrified to ask women out and being cautious to not begin abusing alcohol and drugs like my dad, sister, and brother had done. However, my fears about partying were dissipating as I moved through school.

I wanted to go to college. My interests at the time were women, beaches, and sunshine, so I applied to the University of Florida. The admissions office put me on the waiting list, and I didn't know what that meant. So, I applied to the local college, Towson State University. I was geared towards attending Towson State because I heard the school was known for having more women than men and for partying.

Great Opportunities Inside Difficulties

My senior picture in 1986 as I was deciding what college to attend based on the criteria of sunshine, women, and good times.

Since I was going to Towson State, I decided that I would try and play football. I had done well playing football my senior year of high school and thought it would be a fun thing to do at college. However, as it turned out, I fell back into the same trap of not taking responsibility for opportunities in my life. I didn't call the school to talk to them about walking onto the football team. Since I hadn't taken any action the summer before my freshman year, I planned to try out during the spring semester when I got to school. Once I got to college though, I decided it was more fun to party and chase women than it was to do the work it would take to make my desire of playing football come to life.

I met some great friends in college and had a good time

my freshman year. I have crazy stories about goofy things I did on campus with friends, while drinking and on spring break. Those are good memories. I had to keep a 2.0 grade point average (GPA) to keep a monetary scholarship I received for having asthma. I got a 2.1 and 2.3 GPA my freshman year due to focusing on partying and my overall lack of sense of responsibility.

Excited about going back for my second year.

Strange Behavior

After my car accident, in the summer of 1988, I had gone to Northern Ireland and worked at a YMCA summer camp for kids. I was there for two months and made some great friends. There were camp counselors there from many other countries and it was a great experience.

I met a girl from Northern Ireland there who had come to the camp with some kids from a nearby city. I grew fond of her. We exchanged addresses when she left the camp, and we wrote one another several times when I went back to the

Discovering Faith That Works

United States. We spoke about meeting again, her coming to the United States or me going back to Northern Ireland, but we were nowhere near firming up plans to do that.

In 1989, after the spring semester at Towson ended, I went home to my parents' house and worked at my landscaping job. In the beginning of the summer, I got the idea one day that I was going to fly to Northern Ireland and surprise this girl I met. To do this, I would have to fly to England first. I didn't have much money, but I could buy a one-way ticket. I called five travel agencies and they all told me clearly that if I flew to England with a one-way ticket that England would not let me into the country. However, I kept calling and finally spoke to a travel agency that told me that there would be no problem with me buying a one-way ticket. With that being said, I flew to London and I was detained at the airport. After being in the airport for a number of hours, I was taken to a deportation center. The deportation center was much like a jail and everyone that I can remember there who were being deported like me was from Africa.

The next morning in England, I got escorted onto the airplane by security and then got escorted off the plane when I arrived back in America. This wasn't a comfortable experience. I remember crying on the way home from the airport when my dad came to get me.

Later that summer in 1989, I talked my mother into getting a loan in her name so I could buy a round-trip ticket to Northern Ireland. I was happy because I was still in the mindset of wanting to surprise my friend. We had talked more after my first attempt and it seemed as though she was interested in me coming at some time in the future. However, just showing up out of the blue the second time didn't turn out to be the best idea. The obvious reason was I never told her I was coming. Secondly and just as importantly, I didn't have enough money to support myself in Northern Ireland for two weeks if things didn't go well.

My female friend was surprised that I came, wasn't very friendly after our initial greetings, and became almost rude after that. She lived in a small town and I soon found out that she was dating another gentleman in that town, a professional cricket player.

After I left her town in Northern Ireland, I stayed at a youth hostel in Dublin for over a week. It was okay for several days, but it wasn't much fun when I ran out of money. After not eating for more than a day, I sold my leather jacket to pay for food and my stay at the hostel. I may have been in my early twenties, but I should have thought through both of my trips to Northern Ireland before I left.

Since I had gone back to school after my car accident, my grades were better, and I was getting mostly A's and some B's. In the winter of 1989, I got inspired by the idea that I wanted to attend Brown University, an Ivy League college in Providence, Rhode Island. I had wanted to go to prep school when I was young, but it wasn't in my family's budget to send me there. I also never pursued any alternative steps to go there, which most likely would have worked, like contacting the prep school and seeking a scholarship to try and make my desire to go to prep school come to life.

I liked what I read about Brown's liberal approach to choosing a major and I saw a cool looking guy in a magazine that went there. I know it was a wish to go there, but I wasn't afraid to dream nor take steps to see if there was a way that I could get in. So, I applied to the college, visited the campus with my parents, and sat in on a class while I was there. I didn't get in when I applied.

In the beginning of the summer of 1990, I was lying on my bed in Maryland and I decided the best way for me to get into Brown was for me to get up, get into my car, and drive there to live. I honestly felt at that moment, since this desire to go to Brown was so real and appealing to me, that this was the right thing to do. Without informing my parents, at whose home I was currently living, I packed a small bag and left for Providence. I had gas money and 35 dollars.

Miraculously, not long after I arrived in Providence, I got an apartment. The apartment was several blocks away from the Brown University campus. Within several days, I got a job as a dishwasher at a coffee shop right next to the university bookstore. After some time, I met a nice lady there, whom I dated several times. I was also having fun playing basketball at the outdoor basketball court next to my apartment.

While I was at Brown, all the answers to my problems didn't surface. This was true even though this dream of attending Brown had been so magical in my imagination. The reality was I hadn't gotten any closer to being admitted to Brown. I was losing my apartment, because the student at Brown whom I was subletting from was coming back to school. Furthermore, the genuinely nice woman I had met was going back to college in a different state. So, I decided to leave Rhode Island and come back to Maryland.

As I was driving back to Maryland, I ran out of gas. Luckily, I was close to Baltimore. It was late at night and I had to call a friend of mine I went to college with at Towson State. He was nice enough to get out of bed after midnight and help me get gas.

In the fall of 1990, I attended classes at Towson State, but in the winter of 1990, in another not well-thought-out decision, I decided to take my student loan money, leave school in the middle of the semester, and move back to Rhode Island. I had applied to Brown again and didn't get in, yet I'd continued to romance the idea that being at Brown would solve all of my problems.

This trip didn't go as well as the last one. I got an apartment; however, I didn't find work, felt lonely and disconnected, and had to borrow money from my grandmother to get back to Maryland. My life was becoming more and more unmanageable. However, I didn't realize this. When I wasn't in Rhode Island or Towson, I remember long patches of time where I lived at my parents' house and did nothing productive.

In January of 1991, when I was twenty-two years old, I got the opportunity to move back to Towson and live with a friend of mine from high school. I got a job working as a dishwasher. I wasn't currently in school at Towson State because I'd been placed on academic probation for failing my classes when I left school for Rhode Island in the middle of the fall semester.

In February of 1991, I went to a bar with some friends of mine. At the bar, I met a lady who invited me to attend a concert with her several days later. She was attractive, seemed nice, and this sounded like a fun thing to do.

As I drove to meet her the night of the concert, everything inside me was telling me to turn around and go back home. I'd never had such a strong intuitive feeling like this before. I remember stopping at a store and being painfully perplexed by what to do. In not knowing what to do, I picked up my new friend and we went to the concert. I had fun at the concert, but this feeling that we shouldn't be together never went away. Over the next several weeks and months, I tried to suppress this feeling by trying to distract myself. However, I would be in her apartment and know I had to leave. I would tell her that for some reason I felt bad inside about us and I couldn't see her anymore. I remember at least two times, I left, drove down the street, parked my car in the grocery store parking lot, sat there for several hours, got lonely, and then drove back and asked her if we could get back together again. She took me back every time.

I don't know why I had this uncomfortable feeling. It wasn't as simple as my friend was bad for me or that she was a terrible influence on me and was getting in the way of my life of good purpose. She was a nice person. She was a college graduate, didn't abuse alcohol or drugs, and worked full time pursuing a career in fashion, which was what she studied in college. I, on the other hand, was on academic probation from college, was a fourth-year sophomore, and did not have a major. I worked part time as a dishwasher, wasn't a stable individual, and was by this time an addict.

Three months after we met, she discovered she was pregnant. When she called me at work and told me, I remember being extremely excited. I was twenty-three and this felt like the happiest moment in my life. She didn't sound happy and didn't want to tell her parents that she was pregnant. She wanted to get an abortion.

I didn't want her to. The main reason was because I was extremely excited about the opportunity to be a father. Furthermore, we didn't have the money to pay for the abortion. However, after several days, I asked my father for the money to pay for the abortion and he gave it to me.

Since the time my girlfriend discovered she was pregnant, we began arguing. She began acting for the first time like she didn't want to be involved in our relationship any longer. With all of this going on, I chose not to come to the doctor's appointment when she got the abortion. I was upset about our relationship ending and about her getting the abortion.

After the abortion, I attempted to call her and visit her, but she didn't want to talk to me. In the midst of me harassing her to get back together, I drove to her apartment, ran upstairs, woke her up, and told her that I was going to drive to Ohio and tell her parents that she had gotten pregnant. Several weeks later, I kicked on her front door trying to open it. She was inside, and I remember seeing the scared look on her face through the living room window. My rationale for kicking on the door was that, I felt, if I could get inside, I could talk her into getting back together with me.

While I was kicking on her door, her neighbor came out and told me to go home. We were friends and played basketball together. The police came later that evening and told me to go home. However, I couldn't let go. One afternoon after this, I remember driving to the police station in Cockeysville near my ex-girlfriend's house. Honestly, I remember hoping that they would have someone there who could help me let go of trying to get back together with my ex-girlfriend. I told the police in desperation that I wanted to break into my ex-girlfriend's apartment and get some of my belongings out of there. The police officer told me, in a blunt matter-of-fact kind of way, that if I broke into her house to get my belongings, they would arrest me. I realize now I didn't do a good job of expressing my feelings that day to the police. I wanted help terribly to know how to let go and get peace of mind, but I didn't know how to ask for help.

Eventually, my ex-girlfriend filed two criminal charges against me. The first charge was for "breaking and entering." This was for opening the unlocked door of her apartment, running upstairs, and telling her that I was going to drive to Ohio and tell her parents about the pregnancy. The second charge she filed was for "attempted breaking and entering." This charge was for kicking on her front door.

At the first court hearing, the judge told me that "there were more fish in the sea" and to basically get over my ex-girlfriend. I was bothered by him saying that. However, the disposition of the case that day was postponed for me to get a psychiatric evaluation.

Several weeks later, I went to the appointment to be evaluated by the court psychiatrist. The evaluation report I received from the doctor after the appointment, in my assessment, didn't state that I had a mental illness or any psychiatric problems. However, I thought the court psychiatrist had been rude to me when I met with him in his office. So, after I got the evaluation report, I wrote him a letter cursing him out.

This isn't the first time that I'd written someone an inappropriate letter. I'd written at least two nonsensible letters before this. Earlier that year, I'd written a letter to the boss I began working landscaping for in the summer after high school. He was incredibly good to me and had become a close friend of mine. He and his family came to see me in the hospital several times after my car accident and he allowed me to work whenever I wanted to. Nevertheless, I had written him an extremely critical, confrontational letter about an ill-sided opinion I had regarding the way he spent his money. This letter didn't go over well and tremendously strained our friendship.

I had also written a letter to the dean at the time of Brown University. I was mad that I hadn't got into Brown and that my dream of attending Brown hadn't solved all my problems. I'm not proud of this letter. I don't remember everything I wrote in it, but I do remember some of the things I said were extremely inappropriate.

Great Opportunities Inside Difficulties

At this time, I was back living at my parents' house and often didn't have money to pay for the Bay Bridge toll when I was traveling back and forth from the Eastern Shore to Towson. The procedure at the bridge, if you didn't have the money to pay the toll, was that you would be directed to pull over to the side of the road and wait for the police to come and give you a citation. After having done this several times, I began to just drive off when I was waiting for the police to come.

Since my accident, I was increasingly exhibiting irrational behavior as time progressed. I may have been lazy and irresponsible at times when I was younger, but I had done well in high school and had never gotten into any trouble before my car accident. I had never made irrational, spontaneous decisions before like traveling back and forth to Northern Ireland twice with no money, or moving to Rhode Island twice, impulsively, without thinking things through before I left. Furthermore, I had never tried to kick someone's door open, drive off when I was waiting for the police to come, nor written inappropriate and irrational letters without considering the consequences.

Hope

"Hope itself is like a star- not to be seen in the sunshine of prosperity and only to be discovered in the night of adversity."

– Charles Haddon Spurgeon

Oblivious to me, the state of my mental condition was impairing the way I was processing reality. I was also attempting to cope with life by abusing alcohol and using other addictions. Both problems may have had minimal consequences at first, but now they'd grown to a place where I was harming myself and others with my actions.

My next court date after the psychiatric evaluation, I

had to borrow a friend's car to get to court. My car wasn't working, and I didn't have enough money to get it fixed. On the way to court, I got the strangest idea that the best thing for me to do was not go to court. This idea was confusing to me at first because I had never had a court case before nor ever failed to appear at a court hearing. However, the more I thought this idea through, it became clear to me that the best thing for me to do at that moment was to turn the car around and go back home.

I felt rebellious at first by not going to court, and then I realized that it would be good for me to get arrested and go to jail. I had begun thinking that the reason I was having difficulties in my dating relationships was that I was too passive. I believed that if I went to jail for several days, I would learn how to be more assertive.

When I got home from driving to court, I decided the best action for me next was to write a letter to the judge from my first court hearing telling him what I thought. I was still angry from what this judge had told me in court, at my first hearing, that "there were more fish in the sea" and my letter was full of curse words. As I got to the end of the letter, I decided to state that I was going to kill the judge. I felt saying this to the judge would be the best way to assure myself that I would get the opportunity to go to jail.

After I sent this letter, I remember walking down the

street in the center of the small town I grew up in. I felt a sense of empowerment by placing the letter in the mail. I'm sure, deep down inside, it made me feel like I had control over my life when it was evident by my actions that this wasn't true.

After I wrote the letter, I attempted to turn myself into the police for thirteen straight days. Every time I would go to the police station, they told me that they couldn't arrest me because I wasn't in their computer system yet. On Nov. 21, 1991, the fourteenth day after I wrote the letter, I was lying on my bed at my parent's house when the state police arrived. The police officer who arrested me was friendly.

My experience being incarcerated went downhill from there. The police officers that met me at the Bay Bridge and in Baltimore County weren't friendly like the officer that picked me up at my parents' house. The booking station wasn't fun, nor was the detention center. After being in jail for several days, I went in front of the judge I had threatened for the final hearing on the first charge of "breaking and entering."

The truth was that I was a surfer looking college kid that had never been in trouble before. I'm sure that I never would have set foot in jail for these charges if I hadn't made things worse by not appearing at court and then threatening the judge. With that being said, the judge sentenced me to three years in jail with all but six months suspended. He told me to sit in jail for some time and then to file a motion to have my sentence modified and that he would entertain the thought of doing so.

When I got back to jail from court, I decided that the next best thing for me to do was to write more threatening letters to judges in Baltimore County. I even wrote a letter cursing out the police officer at the police precinct where I first got processed. I thought he acted rude and arrogant and I wanted to let him know.

My present reality was that I currently resided on a dimly lit, isolated jail quad and slept with thirty other inmates in a dorm room. I looked up at security guards sitting in a thick, smudged plexiglass booth. However, writing the letters made me feel better. With that in mind, I tried to write as many letters as possible because it made me feel like I was more in control of my new world, where I had little control.

I got additional criminal charges for writing all these letters. I got charged with multiple counts of "threats on state officials." For these charges, I was taken from the detention center to the Towson police precinct again to get processed. I remember seeing the same police officer there I saw the first time. The one I had just written the derogatory letter to. When I saw him this time, he must have received my letter because he acted like he wanted to fight me.

I was in denial that I was experiencing any direct consequences from these actions I was taking. I didn't know I was suffering from a mental illness, nor that I was using alcohol and other addictions to cope with life. I wasn't happy but I felt like a free spirit. I felt like I could I do anything I wanted to do. The truth is, I had never been free before going to jail.

I was in the Baltimore County Detention Center for almost nine months. It wasn't a fun experience. I got the opportunity to see how life could be so hard for other people and to be able to experience a small part of that myself. Honestly, before going to jail, I never realized that life could be this difficult.

In jail, I shaved off my surfer looking long hair and got a crew cut. I also got a jail house tattoo inscribed on my chest that read "The Motherfucking Cult." Before, everyone had always given me money when I asked for it and made things easy for me. However, no one would bail me out of jail, and I asked a lot of people. My biggest memory of the detention center was that it was closed-in like a box, a lot of people wanted to intimidate you, and I didn't care for most of the people that I had to hang out with all the time.

While I was in jail, my lawyer advised me to file a plea of "not criminally responsible" (NCR) for the charges of the threats I made on the judges. The plea of NCR is an adopted version of the older plea of "not guilty by reason of insanity." My lawyer told me that I could withdraw this plea at any time.

Great Opportunities Inside Difficulties

After agreeing to my lawyer's advice to plead NCR, I received another psychiatric evaluation from the same Baltimore County court psychiatrist that I had written the derogatory letter to after the first time he evaluated me. This time, he concluded that I did have a significant mental disorder and that, in his medical opinion, he recommended that I receive further psychiatric testing to see if I was "not criminally responsible." Pursuant to his recommendation, I was evaluated at Clifton T. Perkins, the state maximum security psychiatric hospital in Maryland for patients found not criminally responsible and incompetent to stand trial. Most of the individuals at this maximum-security hospital had committed serious crimes.

For the charges I received of threatening the judges, the recommendation the hospital had after their evaluation of me was that I was not criminally responsible. The hospital's diagnosis of my mental condition was that I had what is called Organic Mood Disorder and Organic Personality Disorder because of my car accident. After being in jail for almost nine months, I went to court for the final disposition of the charges for threatening the judges.

At court, before my hearing, my lawyer came back to the bullpen section where I was sitting with the other inmates and told me that it had all been worked out. She stated that she had spoken to the assistant state's attorney in my case and that if I pled NCR, I would be sent to the maximum-security hospital for several weeks, have a dangerous hearing, and then be transferred to a head trauma facility. Taking her counsel, I pled NCR.

I showed up at the hospital several days later in a fancy five-hundred-dollar black suit, in handcuffs. When I told the officer who was admitting me what my lawyer told me, he stated in a blunt, matter-of-fact way that I would be found dangerous and be there "a while." He had worked at the hospital over thirty years.

After being at the hospital for several years, I discovered that one of the patients on my unit was trying to go back to court to fight over something that happened in his court case. After speaking and getting some direction from him, I decided that I would file a petition for post-conviction to go back to court and try and get a new trial on the basis that my lawyer had misrepresented me. I was angry that my lawyer advised me to plead NCR, told me that everything had been worked out, and that I would only be at Perkins for several weeks. By this time, I had been at Perkins for several years, and it wasn't looking like I would be getting out anytime soon. I wanted to go back to court, withdraw my plea of NCR, and get a "normal" jail sentence. I say "normal" jail sentence because where I was currently incarcerated, the only way I could physically be free again was if I could prove to the doctors at Perkins and to the court that I wasn't a danger to myself or others.

There was a problem at that time in me proving that I wasn't dangerous. Since I had become incarcerated, I had created a new identity for myself of someone that didn't take any crap from anyone and who fought all the time. Before I went to jail, I had only been in several fights when I was in middle school, some high school locker room shoving matches, and then a brawl outside of a bar one time in college. I had created this new tough guy identity for myself because I didn't like people trying to intimidate me. My new persona had been born out of fear and in me trying to get people to leave me alone. Along with this, I had a mental illness that was characterized by impaired thinking, poor decision making, being impulsive, and acting before thinking about the consequences.

Since I had been incarcerated, I had been in over twenty fights. I had been moved around in the hospital to every maximum-security ward because of fighting and ended up being placed on the behavior management ward. Every shirt I owned had the sleeves cut off at the shoulders. I shaved my head bald, worked out all the time, talked the dentist at the hospital into giving me a gold tooth, and was convinced that the only way to stop someone from trying to intimidate me was to nip it in the bud by fighting about it. I wrote negative articles in the hospital newsletter, and when a social worker at the hospital told me that I should read the Dale Carnegie book, "How to Win Friends and Influence People," I told her that was ridiculous.

Around this time, I started attending twelve-step meetings at the hospital, not to get anything out of them, but to see friends that I had met at the hospital who weren't on my unit. I was also moving through the process of asking the court to give me a new trial on the basis that my lawyer had misrepresented me. I had contacted the public defender's office to help me, but after six months of waiting, I thought they were taking too long. My friend advised me that I could file the post-conviction petition myself. So, I looked through the law books he gave me and filed the petition. To my surprise and delight, I got a court date in several weeks. I then thoroughly prepared for the court hearing because it was especially important to me. This was good, because it gave me something to do and distracted me from focusing on the problems I saw all around me.

The first day of my court hearing, I called eight witnesses. I felt relieved that things weren't going badly when the court bailiff told me when he was locking me into the holding cell, after court, that he thought I did a better job in court than the assistant state's attorney. On the second day of court, at the end of the hearing, the judge said some things that were very meaningful to me. He told me that I did a good job representing myself and he didn't see why I couldn't get out of where I was currently incarcerated.

"Hope is the sun. It is light. It is passion.
It is the fundamental force of life's blossoming."

–Daisaku Ikeda

I had been going to twelve-step meetings in Perkins now for several months. I started feeling better because I was going to the meetings. I now attended the meetings to hear the stories of the people that came in to speak. I couldn't relate to many of the problems I heard people share about. I never had a wife, family, or career to lose and had never slept under a park bench. However, I could relate to the feelings that people shared in the meetings of having felt hopeless, desperate, and discontented.

Some of these people that came to share at the meetings had been incarcerated in jail before much longer than I had been. Other people that came in to speak had experienced problems in life far worse than I would ever want to have and were now living full lives. They seemed happy and at peace.

I started feeling a sense of gratitude from going to the meetings. One night at a meeting, I received a gift that changed my life. It was the gift of hope. This was more than twenty-six years ago.

That evening, I sat in the cafeteria at the hospital with my shaved bald head, gold tooth, muscles, my shirt with the sleeves cut off at the shoulders, and my tattoo that read "The Motherfucking Cult." Even though I wasn't happy, I was proud of the persona I had created. I could have looked confident and strong on the outside, but on the inside, I felt empty and didn't have any hope. Deep down, I had to have realized that if my sentence weren't overturned in my current post-conviction case, so I could get a set jail sentence, then I didn't know how I could possibly get out of where I was currently incarcerated.

As I sat on the cafeteria seat that evening, I heard the

Great Opportunities Inside Difficulties

speaker say, "it doesn't have to be that way." These are only seven words. In attending twelve-step meetings for a number of months, I had heard many words. However, this evening when I heard that phrase, I was overtaken with a powerful feeling of hope. I hadn't felt this feeling for a long time. The hope I received that night felt so refreshing, powerful, and illuminating. It felt like a powerful flow of energy had rushed into my body and gave me the sensation that I had fallen to my knees even though I was still sitting on the steel cafeteria seat.

After I received hope that night, the best thing I ever did was to believe in it and not let it go. Around this same time, I received in the mail the decision from the judge regarding my post-conviction case. It was in a really thick white envelope. I had waited a long time to receive this decision. I remember very clearly opening the envelope. After I read the line in the paperwork that stated my post-conviction relief had been denied, the very first thought I had was, "maybe I'm the problem." Before then, I had no perception that I played a role in any of the difficulties I was having in my life. I honestly felt that all the problems I was experiencing were because of other people.

My new perspective, and the hope I had received that night, gave me the willingness to place myself in positive situations and do the things right in front of me that could make things better. Whatever those things were: whether it was to talk to someone I thought could help me, volunteer to be a part of a class or a group I thought I could benefit from, or to read a spiritual or inspiring book. Hope, and the positive things I was now doing, allowed me to accept taking psychiatric medicine. Others had told me that the medicine would help me, and it has helped change my life. Every positive step I took gave me more and more confidence that I could come out from under the bad situation I had gotten myself into.

Willingness

Practicing Step Three is "like the opening of a door which to all appearances is still closed and locked. All we need is a key... and it is called willingness. Once unlocked by willingness, the door opens almost of itself and looking through it, we shall see a pathway beside which is an inscription. It reads: 'This is a way to a faith that works.' "

- 12 Steps and 12 Traditions, Step 3

Discovering Faith That Works

After some time with all the positive things I was doing, I was moved from the maximum-security behavioral management ward at the hospital to medium security. I then began to work in the kitchen. With hope and willingness, I realized that I needed to continually do the positive things I did at the very beginning to keep moving forward. I'm glad that I realized this responsibility was mine. With my new outlook on life, I began to discover opportunities that were right in front of me that I had been blind to with my old attitude.

One of these was that I had the opportunity, right then, exactly where I was, to go back to college. This was a process. However, after some time of doing work on my end like completing paperwork, applying to programs that could assist in me paying for school, and in continuing to be plugged in to the positive, hope-filled things I had learned to do in my life, it happened.

I was now on minimum security and was enrolled back in college at Towson State, which was now called Towson University. This was the same school I had attended on and off for five years before I got into trouble. It was now over four years later, and I was back in school with a new attitude and direction in my life.

To get to school, I had to take the van from the hospital into the city. I would get dropped off either at a busy bus stop downtown or at the halfway house I began to visit while I was on pre-release. After some time attending school, I came to a place in my pre-release status where I was able to take the train from the city back to the hospital. I remember getting off the train and walking down the country road back towards the hospital and realizing in my heart and mind that the freedom that hope and willingness had given me on the inside was now taking place on the outside.

I majored in Communication Studies and minored in Theatre at school. I liked the theatre classes. I've always wanted to be a good public speaker. I thought the acting classes would help me do this. However, I have a southern drawl to my voice and after taking four acting classes, I was now having the challenge of reciting Shakespeare's writings in my classes. After a semester of struggling through this, I realized it would be a full-time job for me to get better at speaking Shakespeare, so I decided to drop my minor and only focus on my major, Communication Studies.

Since I didn't know what to do with a Communication Studies degree, a friend of mine suggested that I speak to a guidance counselor at school. The counselor had me take a skills assessment test and advised me to participate in an internship in leadership and government. So, I applied to five internships. I remember one was for the State's Attorney's Office, there were several others I cannot remember, and another internship was for Congressman Joseph Kennedy in Washington, D.C. To my surprise, the only internship opportunity that contacted me back was for Congressman Kennedy. He was the son of the late Robert Kennedy and the nephew of John F. Kennedy.

The halfway house and the hospital made me tell the internship coordinator at the congressman's office about the crimes I'd committed and where I'd been incarcerated. I really wanted this internship and I felt terribly apprehensive about doing this. I remember feeling like I was going to die when I walked into the congressman's office in Washington, D.C. to speak to the internship coordinator. However, after telling these things to her, she looked at me, shrugged her shoulders, and told me that it wasn't that big of a deal. To put it lightly, it was extremely encouraging for my self-esteem to be able to wake up at the halfway house in downtown Baltimore, catch the Marc Train to Washington, D.C., walk across Capitol Hill, and then into the Rayburn House Office Building to intern for Congressman Joseph Kennedy.

The next semester, I was able to do a longer internship for a city councilman in Baltimore City. In doing that internship, I had the wonderful experience of being able to research drug free zones with the assistant to the city councilman. I then had the honor of being able to present that research at a meeting with all the city councilmen at City Hall.

Great Opportunities Inside Difficulties

One class at a time, one day at a time, I was able to graduate. I was able to finish the college education I had begun twelve years earlier and had gone from being on academic probation before I got incarcerated to graduating with honors.

In a conversation, the superintendent at Clifton T. Perkins gave me the idea to go to law school and become a lawyer. I'm not positive if he thought I would take him up on his suggestion, but deep down I was looking for a way to raise myself up as high as I had fallen. With that in mind, I signed up to take a prep class that would help me score better on the Legal Scholastic Aptitude Test (LSAT). The LSAT is the test you need to take to apply to law school.

Nevertheless, in this process of studying, I fell back into the pitfall I had when I was younger of not taking responsibility for opportunities that were right in front of me. I ended up not going to the prep course after two classes because I thought it was too long of a bus ride to get there and that I wasn't getting anything out of the class. I had taken a few LSAT practice tests and had only gotten a few of the questions wrong. Sadly, I failed to grasp the reality that just because I got twenty-four out of twenty-six questions correct, if I ran out of time taking the test of thirty-five questions that wasn't performing well.

When I applied to law school, I was put on the waiting

list and eventually didn't get in. However, I had a mentor in my life at this time who impressed upon me that I had to take responsibility for the things I wanted in life and work for them. Before I started my journey with Hope and Willingness, I used to show up for life without doing the work. This mentor helped me to understand that if I wanted more, I needed to do more. With that in mind, I worked harder than I ever had before to get in to law school.

Action

"I have been impressed with the urgency of doing.
Knowing is not enough; we must apply.
Being willing is not enough; we must do."

- Leonardo da Vinci

    I spent my nights and weekends at the Kaplan LSAT prep test office and was determined to get into law school. I applied to several law schools, one harder than the other. I remember thinking that I was going to go to law school somewhere and I was totally confident that I would get in, because I wasn't going to give up.

I finally learned to take the test with a stopwatch, giving myself ninety seconds on each question, and I did much better. I ended up getting into both law schools the second time I applied and had my choice of which one I wanted to attend. I really applied myself in law school. I cannot stress the importance of the fact that I did well because I continued to do the positive things I had done to get me to this place in my life. I continued to ask for help when I needed it. I went to twelve-step meetings every day, talked with counselors and other positive people regularly, went to the gym daily, and read books that inspired me. Furthermore, I continued to take the medication that was prescribed to me at Perkins, and it continued to help me.

I met many friends in law school and had a wonderful experience. I was learning how to take well thought-out risks and apply myself to my own life. I was getting good results and I was even elected to the student government in law school. After a year of doing this, I thought I could help make things better at the school. So, I ran for student president of the law school in my third year. I didn't win the election. However, I was told I only came up short from being elected by two votes.

Furthermore, the judge who presided over my post-conviction case in the Baltimore County Circuit Court taught one of my law school classes. After class one day, I walked up to him and told him that several years ago he had said some inspiring things to me that really helped me. He looked at me quizzically and asked if I was police officer. I stated no but his question made me smile.

Hope, Willingness, and Action now carried me to a place in my life where my dreams were coming true. More and more I began to believe, from the proof of my outside circumstances, that I could do anything I wanted to do.

"Faith is believing in what you do not see;
the reward of faith is seeing what you believe."

– **St. Augustine**

I know that the struggles from my car accident and the head injury, of having a mental illness, being a recovering addict, and having been incarcerated have only carried within them an equal or much greater benefit. In walking through these challenges, I have been able to embrace Hope and discover the virtues of Willingness and Action. I am profoundly grateful to have these challenges because they make me have to take care of myself. They also make me realize I need other people and God in my life every day. Walking through these challenges has given me the tools to have a rich, full life worth living — one that keeps getting better — as long as I keep doing my part.

Today, through God's grace and with the help of many others, I have been able to successfully treat and manage my mental illness and addiction problems for over twenty years. Having had the quality of my life fall so low before I discovered my problems from the head injury, with mental illness and addiction has given me the determination to take advantage of the opportunities in my life right now and to raise the quality of my life just as high, or higher, than it ever fell.

Great Opportunities Inside Difficulties

My law school campaign poster from 2002 Student Bar Association election.

Happy and excited to receive my law school diploma at the 2003 graduation ceremony.

Story 2
A Real Connection

Belief

"Belief is a wise wager.
Granted that faith cannot be proved, what harm will come to you if you gamble on its truth and it proves false.
If you gain, you gain all; if you lose, you lose nothing."

– Blaise Pascal

The second major struggle I had in my life which taught me that great opportunities lie inside of difficult challenges was not passing the bar exam twice to become a lawyer.

The first time I took the test, I scored high enough on one portion of the test to pass but did not score high enough on the writing portion. I tried harder the second time and still wasn't successful. At the same time, I heard a book mentioned in a conversation between two people. I used my hope-inspired willingness to get the book, which was titled, "The Power of Positive Thinking," by Norman Vincent Peale.

In reading "The Power of Positive Thinking," I was given the awareness to realize that even though I didn't have control over many things that happened in my life, I did have control over the thoughts I impressed upon my mind. It helped me discover that I could change my life by changing what I thought. I embraced many of the ideas in that book and subsequently read many other books written by Norman Vincent Peale and many other authors after that in order to get more of the same message. I was learning how to empower my world with hope again. I repeated day after day (and often minute after minute) the words I read: "I Can if I Think I Can," "Expect the Best and Get the Best," "God and Me are a Majority," "God is Bigger than any Problem that Comes My Way," and that "Nothing is Impossible with God."

Great Opportunities Inside Difficulties

One line I read left the greatest impression upon me. The phrase was, "I can do all things through God who strengthens me." I remember thinking that this phrase is in the Bible and I don't see it helping many people. This idea is a difficult concept to grasp to begin with. I've tried to accept it in the past, but it contradicts so much of what my experiences have been and of what I see around me. However, "The Power of Positive Thinking" and other books I read explained many true stories of other people who have grabbed hold of ideas like this and who have been able to change their lives and the lives of others.

At the time I read this phrase, my primary goal was just to pass the Maryland Bar Exam and become a practicing attorney. I thought I could build upon this idea in the future if it worked out. However, passing the bar exam was the most important thing in my world at that time. I was smart enough to pass and I had done well in law school. However, this reality was not translating into my success.

I wanted to see if this idea, "I can do all things through God who strengthens me" was true. I wanted to see if me truly accepting this idea could somehow translate into my success on passing the bar exam. I rationalized that if I said this phrase and other positive thoughts like this all day long, that if this phrase was true, I should at least be led to some idea or something that would help me. I had learned that me by myself was not enough. All the hope that I had been given had helped change my attitude enough that I was willing to work extremely hard for what I wanted. However, I had worked terribly hard to pass the bar exam but my best idea of how to study and accomplish this goal wasn't working. I consciously repeated the phrase "I can do all things through God that strengthens me" literally all day long at any time possible. I eventually personalized this idea to fit my current situation and changed it into "I passed the Maryland State Bar Exam on February 24th and February 25th of 2005 through God who strengthens me." I said this phrase all day long, along with other phrases like "Think success and get success," "I can if I think I can," and "I do not believe in defeat."

Great Opportunities Inside Difficulties

"It's the repetition of affirmations that leads to belief. And once that belief becomes a deep conviction, things begin to happen."

-Muhammad Ali

As I look back, I can see that in the process of affirming the positive results I wanted and in being willing to go to any lengths to achieve them something happened. I was led in a not apparent, matter-of-fact kind of way into taking a bar exam prep course that was quite different than the way I was used to studying. I had taken a very popular bar prep course the first time I took the bar exam. However, the prescribed method of studying taught by that course didn't deter me away from studying the only way I thought was right. This second prep class I was led to challenged my ideas of what I thought was the only way I had to study to be successful.

During this entire process of preparing for the test, I continued to repeat all day long my affirmations. I wasn't going to let up until I took the test. In another not apparent, matter-of-fact kind of way, I was able to accept the method of studying that was taught in the course that I always thought wouldn't work. All we essentially did in the course was practice taking the test over and over again, specifically the essay portion of the test. I spent hardly any time studying the multiple-choice portion of the test. This may not seem like rocket science that I would benefit from, taking the test repeatedly, especially the writing portion, since that was my weakest area. However, me thinking I am right, as I did with the way I thought was the best way to study, can be my biggest fault. Me accepting a new idea and being willing to change was divine intervention.

I did get incredibly stressed out at the end of my studying. It was four days before the test, and by this time I was overthinking and getting stressed out by repeating my affirmations continously. I remember I was in the law school library on a sunny day. I was taking a break from my studying at the long library desk. I was reading another positive thinking book. As I read this book, I came across another idea that has impacted my life. The book described the image of anxiety placing its hands around your neck and choking the smarts, intuition, and the best out of you.

After I read these words, describing this image, I felt like I could relax. I felt confident in getting up from the desk, packing up my books, and going home. I then felt so much peace in trusting my gut. This was the same guy, me, who had been a test crammer and who spent the first year of law school staying up all night long one day a week and sleeping an average of four to five hours a night the other six days. All I did the next three days before the bar exam was hang out with friends, play basketball, and relax.

I felt peaceful the day of the test. I remember sitting in McDonald's before the test feeling very calm. I did get anxious at times waiting the several months for the test results, but I continued to repeat my affirmations. I flew to Georgia to visit my sister and her family the weekend the test results came out. I remember sitting at the computer desk in her house when I found out that I was successful on the Maryland State Bar Exam. I didn't get what would have been a passing score on the multiple-choice portion of the test, even though

I had the first time I took the test. I didn't do anywhere near as well this time. When I took the test in 2005, they didn't disclose the score of the essay portion of the test; however, I had to have aced that portion this time because this time I passed the Maryland State Bar Exam through God who strengthens me.

I'm glad I didn't pass the bar exam twice and am incredibly grateful that I found myself in the exact circumstances I did when I considered that day when I was beginning to study the third time of whether the bible phrase "I can do all things through God who strengthens me" was really true. I feel blessed to have had these difficulties because these challenges only gave me the opportunity to question for myself whether God was real or not. These exact problems I had gave me the determination to try and find out.

Great Opportunities Inside Difficulties

A hermit was meditating by a river when a young man interrupted him. "Master, I wish to become your disciple," said the young man. "Why?" replied the hermit. The young man thought for a moment. "Because I want to believe in God like you do."

The master jumped up, grabbed him by the scruff of his neck, dragged him into the river, and plunged his head under water. After holding him there for a minute, with the boy kicking and struggling to free himself, the master finally pulled him up out of the river. The young man coughed up water and gasped to get his breath. When he eventually quieted down, the master spoke. "Tell me, what did you want most of all when you were under water." "Air!" answered the young man. "Very well," said the master. "Go home and come back to me when you want God as much as you just wanted air."

An Adapted Buddhist Fable

Having these problems allowed me to do everything I thought I could possibly do to bet on faith and to trust God with something that was very dear to me in passing the bar exam. In this process, unbeknownst to me, I was able to change. I was able to do something I thought would not work. I studied less, was able to relax more, and had the privilege to be able to trust God and myself when I stopped studying three days before the test. The most invaluable benefit I received from having had these problems is that they allowed me to have in my heart, in a very deep way, a real experience with God. No one can take that away from me.

The concept of Belief, in me having worked so hard to trust God, has only given me the strength to fight on in other struggles I face today, because I know believing in God works.

Great Opportunities Inside Difficulties

June 14, 2005 certificate of admittance to practice law in the State of Maryland by the state's highest court, the Maryland Court of Appeals.

Story 3

Learning to Love Myself

<u>*Courage*</u>

"Courage is the most important of all virtues because without courage you can't practice any other virtue consistently"

– Maya Angelo

The third difficult challenge I walked through which has only made me realize that there are blessings inside of difficulties was dating before I met my wife.

I don't know how I got so shy and insecure at this time in my life. I was in my early thirties. Maybe it was because I felt shame about my past. Maybe it was because I wasn't drinking alcohol or using any other addiction to try and hide my uncomfortableness while I was trying to date. Whatever was going on inside of me, it was extremely difficult for me to allow myself to be vulnerable enough to try and date when I graduated college and was at law school.

I had taken a lot of time off from dating because I was trying to work on myself. However, after several years of doing this, I was realizing that I wanted to share my life with someone else. I was becoming more successful in my life, yet I knew whether it was money or other successes the key to a rich life for me was going to be sharing these things with someone else.

Even though my life had changed so much, it was important for me to keep following my hope and to keep moving forward. I was getting so much out of reading the positive thinking books I had spoken about, like "You Can if You Think You Can" and others. However, reading these books and believing everything they said was placing me in a difficult situation. It was making me come face to face with my fears and presently, at this time in my life, the greatest fear I had was opening myself up to someone I wanted to date and possibly being rejected. I was now constantly being presented with two paths to travel; one was the fear I knew so well, and the other was the great uncertainty of being vulnerable.

I remember very well one experience I had that demonstrated the crossroads I was at. This evening, I was leaving law school and was walking to my car. As I walked past the front of the building, I passed this extremely attractive fellow law student I wanted to ask out. She was in the class one year ahead of me. I had become very outgoing in other areas of my life, was in the student government at school, and had talked to her causally several times. A friend of mine who I played basketball with was in her section. He explained to me that she was not available. He said she didn't date fellow law students but only went out with pro-athletes and people like that.

I remember when she walked past me that night, she looked at my face and smiled. I kept walking and when I turned the corner to walk toward the parking lot, I stopped and sat on a bench. I was now anguishing over the decision I had to make. I could choose fear, not do anything, and allow my fears to stop me from living the life I wanted to, or I could choose Courage and Action and allow myself to be vulnerable and conquer my fears.

Discovering Faith That Works

After sitting there for fifteen minutes perplexed, I realized the best choice for me to make was to get up, be brave, and go back into the law school to see if I could find her. I was soon able to see her at the law library. I walked over to her, asked her if she wanted to go out sometime, and she gave me her phone number. I even called her and she called me back. No flourishing romance came out from this, but I was able to take one great big leap of faith in conquering the fears that had previously paralyzed me.

"Do what you fear, and the death of fear is certain"

– Ralph Waldo Emerson

Great Opportunities Inside Difficulties

In confronting these fears, I ended up acquiring a priceless gift. In twelve-step groups, they commonly refer to this phenomenon as "being comfortable in your own skin." I had at that time been involved in twelve-step groups for more than six years. In that process, I had taken many of the actions suggested in those groups and made many strides towards feeling better about myself and being comfortable with who I was. However, nothing I have done in my life before or after this has given me the truest sense of this feeling than walking through these fears when I was dating at this time in my life. Honestly, after some time in doing this it was more important for me to take the action of conquering my fears than getting a date or going out with whoever I asked.

This challenge blessed me in many more ways besides having this wonderful feeling of being comfortable in my own skin. I am happily married today and have been with my wife for over fifteen years. I know that if I hadn't chosen courage many years ago and had not walked through the paralyzing fears and insecurities I had, I wouldn't be where I am today. In going through this process, I discovered the confidence I needed to be able to stand my ground when difficult times arose in a relationship instead of either running away or suffocating the other person.

Discovering Faith That Works

On July 24, 2009, reading this poem I wrote to my wife at our wedding:

I am very fortunate and truly blessed to be able to stand here today with you.

Yet the truth must be confessed that God's grace is the only clue

That could explain me being given the honor to share my life with you.

For there is no duty or act I could have performed

That would have rewarded me with the privilege of being able to be with you.

Irena, today I want the whole world to know that

I am living my dream beside you.

Great Opportunities Inside Difficulties

Before I got into trouble, at twenty-three, with the problems I have described, I had many short-term relationships but none that lasted any longer than six months. Courage, the confidence that came from that, and working on myself has allowed me to have the long-lasting, healthy, committed, stable relationship I have had with my wife for not six months but over one hundred and eighty months. That is a miracle.

I also had to work so hard on changing myself, by doing much more work than I ever cared to, that I became determined to not settle for less and be blown away by the woman I would eventually marry. My wife is very pretty to me, but the most wonderful fact is that she is just as beautiful on the inside to me as she is on the outside. I never would be at this place in my life if I had not learned how to be courageous.

Discovering Faith That Works

My wife, Irena, on our wedding day fixing her hair before we got married.

My wife with cake on her nose, thanks to me, at the wedding reception at our home.

Story 4
Grace I Couldn't See

Visualization

"Visualization is the human beings' vehicle to the future – good, bad or indifferent. It's strictly in our control."

- Earl Nightingale

Discovering Faith That Works

The fourth blessed struggle I had to walk through that showed me that great opportunities are inside of difficult challenges was the story of how I started my own law practice.

In 2006, my first job as an attorney was working at a non-profit quasi-governmental agency in Baltimore City. I was hired to be a family advocate attorney. The agency I worked for assisted residents that were being relocated through the process of eminent domain. This involved the city acquiring their homes and moving the residents to other communities. In my role as a family advocate attorney, some of the services I provided were case management and others were getting the residents connected to legal services to resolve their legal issues. I worked at this job for over five years. This job was not a good fit for me nor was I a good fit for it.

By this time, my wife and I had bought a home and had taken on other financial responsibilities. Even though this job was not a good fit on either end, I needed the income and was too scared to make any changes. The job was also remarkably busy and had a lot of stress. In all of these outside pressures and new responsibilities, I lost focus on taking care of myself and in using the tools that had gotten me this far.

For the previous nine years, I had gone to approximately seven to ten twelve-step meetings a week. I was now only going to about one and a half meetings a week. I felt challenged by my job situation, but in not taking care of myself I was unable to realize that it was my responsibility to address these challenges. I honestly didn't know what to do. I felt stuck and nominated myself to be a victim. I eventually lost my self-respect. In doing this, I became disempowered. I had gone up the escalator from being incarcerated for five years, graduating from law school, and meeting my wife, and now I was going down the escalator and didn't how to get off. I lost belief in myself and struggled to continue to believe in hope. Even though this was over ten years ago, this is still a very painful memory.

In hindsight, I realize I was too concerned with what was going on around me and wasn't paying attention to my inner voice, which was extremely upset. I didn't appreciate how important it was for me to listen to what was going on inside me. Thankfully, even though I stopped doing many of the positive things that got me this far, I never quit on hope. I hung in there even though I didn't know what to do. I read my positive thinking books. I prayed to the concept of God I had at that time. I had read that it was always too soon to quit, and I knew that was the truth. Eventually, after multiple years of internally feeling like I was being dragged behind a bus, I stumbled into being willing to take some actions that worked.

At this time, I was seeing a therapist. He helped me begin to meditate on feeling better about myself in my work situation. He created a guided meditation that I would listen to that involved visualization. I had read in one of my positive thinking books that visualizing was the powerful next step in obtaining positive outcomes in your life. This concept made sense to me because it was easy for me to conceptualize how worrying is using the power of our imagination in the opposite direction. Visualizing had actually been one of the powerful hope-filled concepts I used when I was dating at the time I met my wife.

I met my wife at work. When we met, I had first read how powerful visualizing was supposed to be. In working together, my wife and I soon discovered that we had this wonderful connection. We made each other laugh and we felt comfortable with one another. We had gone to a dance together, had a magical time, and she had become very dear to me. However, this was not a simple, blissful love story because where we worked, you weren't allowed to date people you worked with. Furthermore, my wife and I were doing this come close, move back relationship dance that took some time to adjust to.

However, in the midst of all of this, it became so natural for me to take the advice of the visualization books I was reading and to just lie in bed at night and picture my wife lying in bed next to me. There was nothing sexual in these thoughts I had; it just felt so soothing and reassuring to visualize myself holding onto her in bed every night. I would then

Great Opportunities Inside Difficulties

in the middle of the day picture her sitting in my car holding my hand and us walking down the street together. I pictured these things in my mind long before they became reality.

Now as I found myself in the middle of these horrific challenges at work, it was five years later, and my wife and I were married. Pondering upon the thought that visualization could be the next step in feeling better in my work situation, I asked my therapist about this. I wanted to know that if I wrote down the perfect job for me he could put that into a guided meditation. He thought that was a great idea. So I took the time to write down what I thought would be the perfect job for me.

I listed all the things I wanted to do in a job. At the position I currently had, I wasn't going to court as much as I wanted. When I did go, what I did was very limited. The truth for me was that I had always enjoyed representing people in court. I had learned that I loved doing this in law school. I enjoyed this at my current job in the limited times I was able to do this.

I created a visualization where I pictured myself walking into the courthouse, being respected for the job I was doing, arguing cases in the Circuit and District Courts, and speaking to other lawyers in helping clients resolve their matters. I imagined myself doing challenging things that interested me, being happy with the work I did, and being respected by my peers. I was also sick of sitting in the cubicle desk I had at my current job. I imagined my own personal office with me inside it.

When I was done, we placed the description of my perfect job in a CD. I listened to it every day, sometimes more than once. I remember when I would listen to the recording it felt as though I was actually experiencing the story I created. When I finished listening, very often you couldn't tell me that I hadn't experienced the story I just heard.

In the process of me being disciplined in listening to my visualization, I soon discovered that the company I was working for was downsizing and I and several other people were being laid off. I remember telling my therapist that I felt I was going to get a new job within a month. He looked at me with disbelief. Even though I was getting laid off, I continued to do all the things I had begun to do to take better care of myself. I started going back to more twelve-step meetings and putting myself first.

One week after I was laid off, I saw a guy I went to law school with. We used to play basketball together. I asked him if he knew of any job opportunities. He advised me to contact a private attorney I had never heard of before. In my job search, I had been looking for jobs with the government that I thought would be more secure and have reasonable working hours. I never desired to work for a private law firm

Great Opportunities Inside Difficulties

because I feared that I would have little control over balancing my life in this type of environment. With that in mind, I applied for jobs at the City Law Department and the Attorney General's Office. However, no opportunities had come out of these jobs I was applying for.

Several days after the conversation with my law school friend, I was speaking with several friends of mine, who were not lawyers, in a parking lot. Upon hearing of my job search, they both gave me the name of the same lawyer the other guy gave me, even though I hadn't mentioned this lawyer's name to them. One of these friends gave me the lawyer's phone number. The other friend said he knew the lawyer well and would let him know I'd be calling.

Since I had gotten laid off, I got in the practice every morning after meditating and listening to my visualization CD to do the hardest thing first in my job search. I knew action was the key, so I left the conversation, walked to my car, and called this lawyer they spoke of. I got his answering machine and left a message. I never heard back from him.

Several days later, I went to visit the office of an older attorney who was a mentor of mine. He was helping me with my job search. I'd never been to this lawyer's office before. I mentioned to him the name of the private attorney that my three friends had given me. His face lit up. He got very excited and told me that he knew this lawyer and his father well. He told me their office was in the building right next door to his. He then picked up the phone and called the attorney's father and left a message.

These coincidences were too much for me. I did have lunch plans, but I remember turning my car around and going home to edit my resume. When I was done, I drove to this private attorney's office. I opened the door, and no one was there at the secretary's desk. I stood there for a moment, and then heard someone in the hallway. As I approached the hallway, I ran into this great big Greek guy.

This was the attorney everyone told me about. I showed him my resume and told him I was looking for a position. I told him four people had given me his name. After looking at my resume, he told me that he wasn't hiring anyone. However, he told me that he had an empty office upstairs and if I wanted to start my own law practice, he would let me rent the office free for several months and refer me some cases. His father came out and both men were very encouraging to me about starting my own law practice.

I had received a severance package from being laid off from my last job. I still had most of that money. I spoke to my wife, another mentor of mine, and my therapist about this. They all felt I had nothing to lose by taking this risk, going out on my own and starting my own law firm.

Today it has been over nine years, and I still own my own

law firm. This story is such a dear memory to me because I was only out of work for two weeks from the time I got laid off until the day I started my own practice. So many magical, coincidental things happened in that process. If you had given me a multiple-choice test when I first started my job search and told me to choose what job I wouldn't have gotten, it would have been starting my own law firm. The concept of me doing this was nothing I could have conceived of at that time. Occasionally, I would daydream of winning the lottery, becoming financially independent, and starting my own law practice. However, the reality of what occurred is out of this world. The most beautiful thing is that soon after starting my own practice, I was doing ninety-seven percent of the things I wrote down on paper and put into my visualization.

The great benefits I feel I've received in walking through this struggle of getting busy with life, losing my focus, and not taking care of myself is that I've been able to reset my priorities. Today and every day since this painful experience, I've been committed to putting myself first. I now make it a priority to pray, exercise, and go to a twelve-step meeting every day. I have friends that laugh about how rigid I am in doing this, but I know how easy it was for me to lose my focus on taking caring of myself, so now I make it the center of every day.

Also, in having to walk through this difficult time, I was

able to discover again the power of the faith-filled concept of visualizing exactly what you want in life and then receiving it. I had done this when I first met my wife. Now I was placed in the exact position where I was able to use this principle again, and the wonderful opportunity of starting my own law firm came into my life.

Finally, a tremendous insight I got out of having gone through this experience is another glimpse of what I feel God is all about. As I stated previously, having the resolve, confidence, and opportunity to start my own law firm was nothing I could have conceived of before it happened. These facts, along with the mind-boggling coincidences that occurred and the faith principle of visualization I learned about, leave me only with the realization that God must want so much more for us then we could ever dream of for ourselves. This idea gives me the hope of needing to continue to push forward in all of my frailties and struggles and reach for God so I can experience again this love I know God has for every single one of us.

Great Opportunities Inside Difficulties

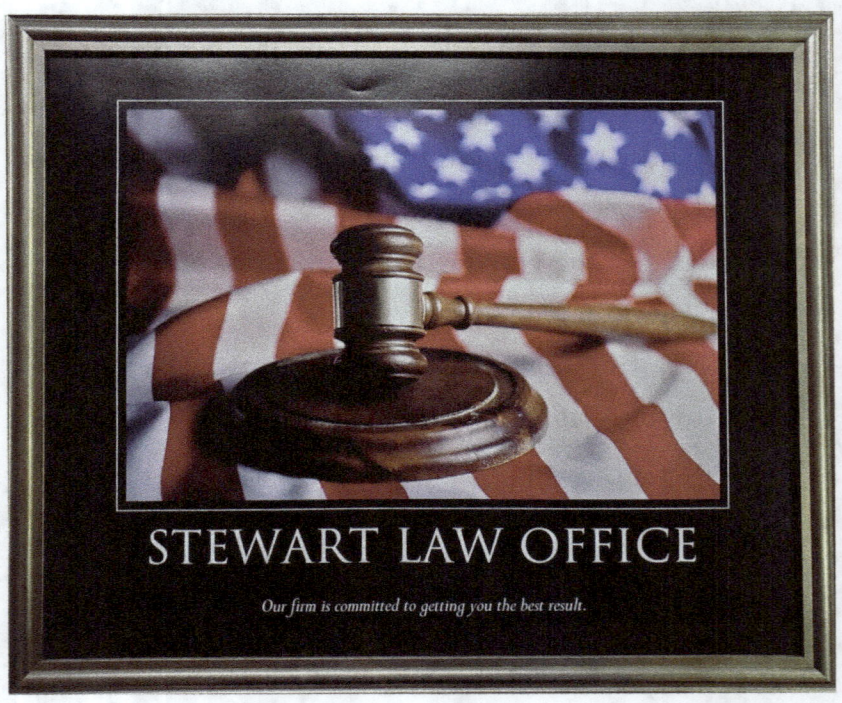

Stewart Law Office picture hanging in my office at my law firm.

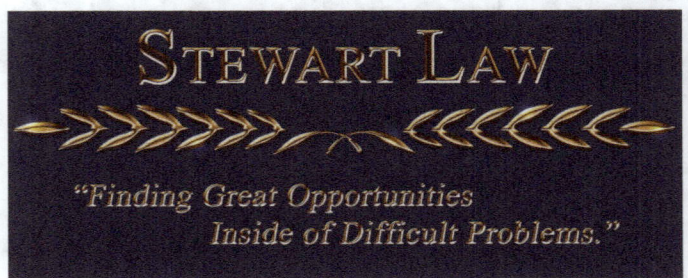

Law Firm logo that mirrors the title of this book and why I like helping people in my profession as a lawyer because I know ... there are "Great Opportunities Inside Difficult Problems."

Story 5
Surrendering to Success

Publishing this Book

"All the art of living lies in the fine mingling of letting go and holding on."

- Henry Ellis

The last precious struggle I have had to walk through in life, which I know only has blessings equal to or much greater than the difficulty, has been publishing this book.

All of the fears and pain I've felt in this journey of publishing this book have made me look at and gain a broader understanding of several other factors of a faith that works. These principles are Acceptance, Humility, Responsibility, Trust, and Surrender.

Acceptance

"Accept — then act. Whatever the present moment contains,
accept it as if you had chosen it.
Always work with it, not against it."

- Eckhart Tolle

When I first started a draft of this book, I was very worried. How could I share this book with anyone else? I'm a lawyer. I own a law firm. My office is two blocks away from the Baltimore County Circuit Court and the majority of my court cases are heard in Baltimore County. In my book, I speak about writing threatening letters to judges in Baltimore County, being incarcerated for five years, being an addict, having a mental illness, and being a patient at Clifton T. Perkins, a well-known maximum-security forensic hospital in Maryland for the criminally insane.

In my struggle to write this book, I read the book, "The Obstacle is the Way," by Ryan Holiday. In his book, Holiday speaks about how inside the obstacles in our lives lay the path for us to travel. I believe this to be true. I truly grasp the idea that if I cannot get around a problem in my life, the great reward must be in having to lean forward and walk through that difficulty or the challenge wouldn't be there. To me, my past only declares this to be true.

However, me not knowing how to handle the challenges of publishing this book had been a problem for me for over seven years. When I was my most authentic self, I knew completing this book and sharing it with others was the right thing to do. I wanted to be brave enough to share these stories about my life without being concerned about the responses of other people. I wanted to be detached and

Great Opportunities Inside Difficulties

have the strength to not let my fear of the opinions of others stop me from being free enough to live the life I wanted to live by publishing this book.

"Because one believes in oneself, one doesn't try to convince others. Because one is content with oneself, one does not need the approval of others. Because one accepts oneself, the whole world accepts him or her."

- Lao Tzu

Humility

"Humility is not necessarily thinking less of oneself. It lies in thinking of oneself less."

- **Anonymous**

In the journey of publishing this book, I've had to digest the fact that the only way I could move forward was to practice humility, and to do that I had to stop thinking about myself all the time. I realized I had to start living a faith that works

Great Opportunities Inside Difficulties

by letting go of trying to protect my position of remaining at the center of everyone else's universe. There is way too much going on down here, on planet Earth, for me to be so concerned about myself when most people do not care because they are too busy living their own lives.

One of the most powerful experiences I've had in all of this is the clear thought I had one afternoon about four years ago. I was in Baltimore City. I had leased a small office in a high-rise office building to devote to completing this book. I would be at times excited with the task of writing the book and other times paralyzed with the fear of sharing it with others. However, one day when I was leaving this office, I had this crystal clear thought. I remember exactly where I was walking when I had this thought that *"my past could be the most perfect thing that ever happened to me."* This is a sobering idea for me, especially after having been paralyzed by the fears of publishing this book for so long and feeling trapped by the experiences of my past.

Not long after this experience, I awoke one day from being so wrapped up in myself to see an incredibly sad sight. I was walking back from my Baltimore City office to my car, and when I turned the corner, I couldn't help but pass by the motionless body of a person lying in the bushes. As I looked closer, it was a fifty-year-old man, passed out, fully dressed in too many clothes on a hot summer day, lying face down in the bushes. In looking past my self-righteousness, I knew that this gentleman is as important in the entire cosmos as I am and that he has been given a purpose in this life as important as any purpose I feel I have. At that moment, he was physically alive but was dead to living the precious life we've all been given.

"No man is an island entirely of itself; every man is a piece of the continent, a part of the main. Any man's death diminishes me, because I am involved in mankind. And therefore never send to know for whom the bell tolls; it tolls for thee."

- John Donne

Great Opportunities Inside Difficulties

There is clearly much more going on down here than me needing to be so concerned about what other people think of me.

Responsibility

"You are not only responsible for what you say but also for what you do not say."

- Martin Luther

Great Opportunities Inside Difficulties

I know in life that some things are my responsibility, and some things are not. I've tried very hard to not write this book. I've tried to figure out how to ignore wanting to write this book and also not wanting to complete the task of doing it. I've tried to figure out how I could publish the book under a pen name and not lose the value of being my genuine self.

The reality is that I have a relationship with God. I feel that in every relationship there is a give and take and some things I need to do to be a part of that relationship. I fall to the fact that I cannot maintain the transparent relationship I care to have with God if I do not publish this book.

"It is easy to dodge our responsibilities, but we cannot dodge the consequences of dodging our responsibilities."

-Josiah Charles Stamp

Trust

"Pray and let God worry."

-**Martin Luther**

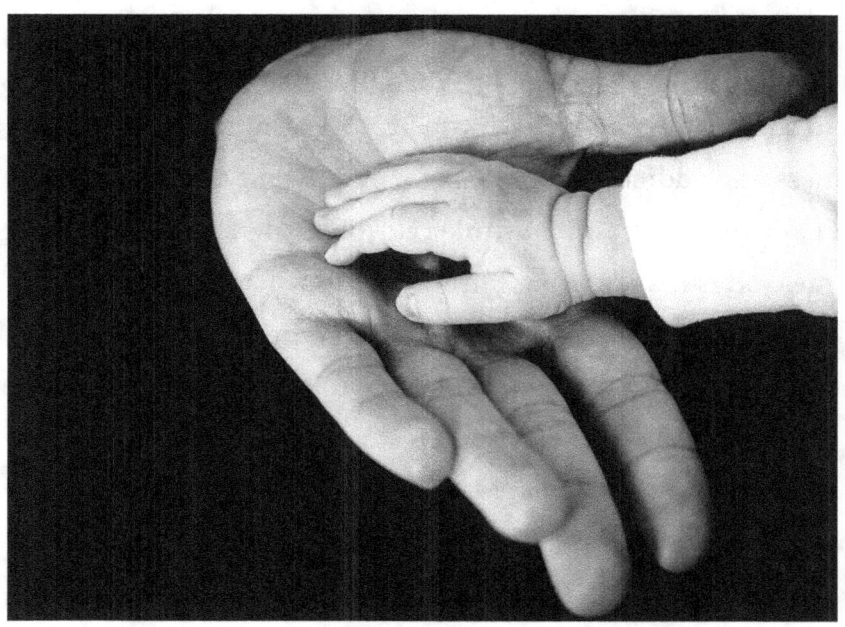

Several months ago, I heard a warm story of a man who had been homeless a number of years ago, estranged from his family, unemployed, and living on the streets of Baltimore City for years. I knew the man casually but didn't know he had these experiences in his past. When I heard him share these things, he was getting ready to meet his daughter and granddaughter for breakfast. He stated that he hadn't seen his daughter for years and had never met his granddaughter.

When I heard him share this, I was overcome with this realization: *How can I not trust God?* A few years ago, I was incarcerated and a fifth-year sophomore in college on academic probation, with untreated mental illness and addiction problems. Today, I am a lawyer, own my own law firm, have a lovely home, wonderful wife, and have been able to successfully treat, with the help of others, my mental illness and addiction problems for over twenty years. I have an inspiring story and multiple real-life experiences that show me God is real and that faith works.

Recently, I heard a different rendition of the famous bible story of how Moses was able to part the Red Sea. I am familiar with the Charlton Heston movie version of what occurred. In the movie, Moses is able to speak to God, wave his rod, the sea opens up, and there is plenty of room to travel. Then all the Israelites walk through safely, and the Egyptians are engulfed as the sea closes around them.

This other version of this same story of Moses parting the sea was from a Jewish reading. The lady who shared the story explained that even though Moses had raised his rod and communicated with God, nothing happened. One man had to be brave and trust God enough to jump into the water and start walking. Only in doing this, did the sea begin to part.

This description of what occurred has been such a powerful image to me. It fits in so much with my past experiences regarding faith, writing this book, and many other current challenges I face. In choosing to jump in the water and start walking, I place myself in a position where all I can do is rely upon and trust God. There is an army behind me; seemingly unchanging, insurmountable challenges in front of me; and a pressing belief that God wants me to keep walking forward even though very often my head goes underwater and the sea level never falls below my shoulders.

I can play this image out in my mind and imagine that after a difficult, scary experience, suddenly the sea level drops from my shoulders to my waist and I finally make it to the other shore. As I walk up onto the beach, I see myself being resentful at God for not parting the sea and making my trip any easier. I am then approached by a fisherman asking me how I got on the beach. When I explain to the fisherman, in a frustrated tone, how I just had to walk from the other seashore to this beach, the fisherman swears that I am lying to him. He then explains to me how the sea I just walked out of is three hundred feet deep in the middle and that my story cannot be true. I then fall back with my hands to my head and realize that even though my journey was difficult, God did for me what I could not do for myself.

Surrender

"I am simply not enough in myself, but in Him I am. This surrender is not weakness, but the only true measure of strength any of us have."

- Aaron W. Matthews

Great Opportunities Inside Difficulties

With all these things having been said, I still have struggled with Humility, Acceptance, Responsibility, and Trust and was still unable to publish this book. I was having several other challenges in my life at the time I was able to complete the book. It was during the pandemic in May of 2020. These struggles involved my business and finances and I had to pray and rely upon God more to address these challenges. I began focusing on the things that were right in front of me. In this process, I began to have the most remarkable experience. I started to realize that completing this book was a priority, and I began to be able to do what I haven't been able to do before by myself. I started feeling God's strength in allowing me to finish this book. Over the last seven years, I had tried extremely hard to implement these eleven principles of a faith that works in order to complete this book, but I had yet been unable to surrender to God's will to do so. Recently it has only been through the remarkable sensation that God was helping me that this book got completed and published.

Discovering Faith That Works

The great benefits I have found so far in publishing this book is in having to accept myself and my past at a deeper level. I also feel in having to walk through all the struggles I have had in publishing this book that I have been blessed to be able to begin the wonderful journey of learning more about how Humility, Acceptance, Responsibility, Trust, and Surrender are characteristics of a faith that works.

In finishing this book, I also began to be conscious of the most amazing sensation. I began to feel that God was doing for me what I haven't been able to do by myself. In concentrating on God more, as I was doing with the other problems I discussed above, it felt as though something that wasn't my normal self was giving me the strength and willingness to complete this book. I've never had this experience before

Great Opportunities Inside Difficulties

and only pray that I can live a life of surrender so that I can be able to do what I feel God desires me to do.

My prayer as I move forward is ...

"God, I pray that you will please help me find the greatest opportunity inside the difficulty of me writing my book, which is your perfect will, and that you will give me the courage, strength, and the willingness to do that."

Closing

In this book, I have shared five stories from my life when I had to walk through difficult problems. These experiences began with me losing hope while suffering from a head injury, with mental illness, addiction, and being incarcerated. I spoke about challenges I faced in passing the bar exam to become a lawyer; dating before I met my wife; starting my own law practice; and in publishing this book. In walking through all of these precious struggles, I've learned so much. I was introduced to eleven concepts of a faith that works. These principles are Hope, Willingness, Action, Belief, Courage, Visualization, Acceptance, Humility, Responsibility, Trust, and Surrender. I know these are characteristics of a faith that works because in discovering these virtues, I have been able to create a new life worth living. Beyond being introduced to these eleven character-building attributes, I've been fortunate enough to realize that inside each difficulty has been a great opportunity, equal to or much greater than the problem I had to face.

I hope some story or phrase in this book has inspired you, the reader, to not give up in the middle of the challenges you are currently facing and to create a new life worth living. Know that you and God can.

"It is always too soon to quit."

- Norman Vincent Peale

Know the five stories in this book were past challenges I walked through. Like everyone else, I presently have the opportunity to discover a faith that works and continues to work in any and all conditions I face. The message in this book has expanded to a weekly podcast called "Great Opportunities Inside Difficulties" that can be found among other places on Anchor at anchor.fm/rue-p-stewart and my website, www.ruestewart.com.

The podcast is a discussion of finding blessings and equal or much greater benefits from having to walk through difficult problems. The discussion includes interviews with many other people who have had to travel different paths but who have also discovered great opportunities inside difficult challenges.

Please join me on social media, my website and podcast as we work together to discover faith that works.

Discovering Faith That Works

About the Author

I am happily married and enjoy spending time with my wife, family, and our dog, Bebe. I use my free time to exercise, watch sports, and read. I'm a divorce attorney and I feel honored to have the privilege to provide people with hope, strength, and legal counsel as they look for God's purpose in having to walk through some of the most difficult times of their lives.